CALIFORNIA GRASSROOTS TOURS

Selected Short Outings

Redwood National Park

by **ERIC J. ADAMS**

A RENAISSANCE HOUSE PUBLICATION

ISBN: 1-55838-135-X

RENAISSANCE HOUSE
A Division of Jende-Hagan, Inc.
541 Oak Street ~ P.O. Box 177
Frederick, CO 80530

Cover Photo of San Diego Bay courtesy San Diego Convention & Visitors Bureau

10 9 8 7 6 5 4 3 2 1

Redwood National Park

Welcome

From the mist-shrouded coast of Big Sur to the barren deserts of the Colorado River basin, California is as rich and diverse as its population of 35 million people. Despite its large population (one in eight Americans is a Californian), travelers can still find plenty of pristine beauty, and natural surprises, as well as man-made delights here.

Take the Pacific Coast Highway. A drive along the cliffs and breathtaking vistas of Highway One reveals a coast remarkably unspoiled. The same is true of the Gold Country, where travelers can pan for illusive treasure under the shade of twinkling Aspen trees.

In the Redwood Country, nature takes a sharp turn upward with Sequoia and Redwood trees that scrape the skies like downtown buildings. Those whose quest is for heights should visit Mt. Whitney, the highest point in the continental United States at 14,494 feet. Travelers seeking the other extreme can travel 90 miles to Death Valley, the lowest point in the U.S. at 282 feet below sea level. At Lake Tahoe, it's possible to slip a quarter in a Nevada-side slot machine, then travel five minutes to a California trout hole that you'd swear had never been fished before.

For urban adventurers, California is a delight. Romantic San Francisco, the aquatic pleasures of San Diego, and the stars of Hollywood, all make it apparent that there are many Californias, each a remarkable place waiting to be explored. For more information about the Californias contact:

California Office of Tourism
P.O. Box 9278, Dept. A1003
Van Nuys, CA 91409 * (800) 862-2543

Contents

Wine World Estates BERINGER VINEYARD

TASTE THE NAPA VALLEY

Ask a Californian to point you to Wine Country and invariably you'll end up in the Napa Valley. This slender 30-mile valley, 50 minutes northeast of San Francisco, is home to some of the world's greatest vineyards, among them Robert Mondavi, Franciscan, Beringer, Christian Bros., and Charles Krug.

From San Francisco take the Golden Gate Bridge north. Turn east on Hwy. 37, then north again on Hwy. 29. From Napa (pop. 62,000) travel north through the charming towns of Yountville, Oakville, Rutherford, and St. Helena until you reach the jewel of Napa Valley, Calistoga. This area has several health spas with hot mineral springs and volcanic ash mud baths. Enroute, stop to sample the seemingly endless varieties of white and red wines. Tasting is usually free, though some wineries charge a nominal fee.

To explore the quieter side of Napa Valley, take Silverado Trail, which runs parallel to Hwy. 29. The views are nicer and the wineries less crowded. Travelers can also rent bicycles in Napa and Calistoga to explore the many side roads, where wineries are located in converted Victorian houses. Several companies offer hot air balloon rides. An historic train runs along Hwy. 29. There is a spectacular geyser in Calistoga, and a variety of companies offer plane, helicopter, or glider rides in the valley.

Sonoma Valley Visitors Bureau HACIENDA WINERY

Relax In Sonoma Valley

Just west and parallel to Napa Valley lies the lush Sonoma Valley, called by Native Americans "The Valley of the Moon." This is a premiere wine growing region with wines that some say rival Napa Valley's production. Although it has more than 33 wineries, Sonoma offers a less crowded wine experience, though the region is rapidly growing in popularity. Sonoma Valley is also home to California's most northerly mission, and is the adult home of Jack London, author of *Call of the Wild,* and *The Sea Wolf.*

For a relaxing day trip by car from San Francisco, take Hwy. 101 north to Hwy. 37, then Hwys. 121 and 12 into the heart of Sonoma. Sonoma Plaza is an old town square, dating to the days when California was Mexican territory. Here, 150 years ago, angry settlers raised the Bear Flag in defiance of Mexican rule.

While in the town of Sonoma, detour onto Old Winery Rd. to two hidden but spectacular wineries, Hacienda and Buena Vista, good stops for a picnic lunch. Continuing on Hwy. 12, follow signs for Glen Ellen and Jack London State Historical Park. The charming towns of Glen Ellen and neighboring Kenwood are home to more distinguished wineries, including Chateau St. Jean and Glen Ellen. For an overnight stay, Sonoma offers a variety of bed & breakfasts, inns, lodges, and hotels. To return to San Francisco, retrace the route or continue on Hwy. 12 to Santa Rosa, then down Hwy. 101.

D. Parker ALONG THE RIVER

Fun On The Russian River

When a beautiful river meets a beautiful ocean, the results are spectacular. At the town of Jenner, the wide mouth of the Russian River meets the Pacific Ocean. Here each evening, travelers gather to watch the sun set over this magnificent spot.

Jenner is just one delight along the Russian River. The area also offers mighty redwood trees, wineries, swimming, boating, fishing and more.

To reach the area, travel up Highway One to Jenner and turn east on Hwy. 116; or take Hwy. 101 north from San Francisco to River Rd., just north of Santa Rosa.

The lazy Russian River is perfect for recreational canoeing. Forestville and Guerneville have boat rental facilities. For travelers seeking a hot afternoon swim, Memorial Beach in Healdsburg and Johnson's Beach in Guerneville both offer large dammed-off swimming areas, complete with wading spots for kids and offshore floats for experienced swimmers. There are also paddle boats, inner tubes, and canoes for rent.

Hikers can trek under some of the state's tallest coastal redwoods, including the 310-foot Parson Jones Tree in Armstrong Redwoods State Preserve near Guerneville. Bird watchers should keep an eye out for rare spotted owls. The best fishing along the river is in the fall when the silver and chinook salmon begin their spawning runs. While here, don't miss the famous Korbel Champagne vineyard for a tour on the art of champagne making and a sampling of fine champagne and wines.

California Office of Tourism DIVING GRAY

WATCH THE WHALES

It's easy to understand what attracts artists and poets to Mendocino, the quaint lumber and fishing village 120 miles north of San Francisco on Highway One. Rugged terrain and Cape Cod-style houses make this an inspiring region.

Passing through the coastal waters nearby are the 40-ton California Gray whales. The best time to watch these majestic and soulful mammals is between December and March as they migrate south from their summer quarters in the Arctic Ocean and Bering Sea to warmer waters near Baja California. This 6,000-mile trip takes the whales three months, and no fewer than 10,000 of them make the annual pilgrimage.

California Grays travel in groups called pods, consisting of three to five individuals. Since the whales are usually found 1/4 to 1/2 mile off shore, travelers need binoculars to catch a glimpse from land. Prime observation spots are Laguna Point at MacKerricher State Park and the Mendocino Headlands. For a closer glimpse of these magnificent creatures, take a whale watching excursion from Noyo Harbor at Fort Bragg.

Don't leave town without stopping by the Mendocino Coast Botanical Gardens or the curious "pygmy forest" in Van Damme State Park, where vegetation is dwarfed due to hostile soil conditions. Here, full-grown pine trees stand one foot tall. To reach Mendocino from San Francisco, travel north on Hwy. 101, then west on Hwy. 128 or Hwy. 20 to the coast.

National Park Service REDWOODS NATIONAL PARK

Dwarfed By Big Trees

California travelers can easily spend a day or a week under the canopy of the tallest trees in the world. From San Francisco, the nearest place to catch a glimpse of the giant redwoods is in Muir Woods National Monument, just off Highway One, 30 minutes north of the Golden Gate Bridge. The coastal redwood belt runs about 500 miles, much of it along Hwy. 101, and varies in width from 1 to 20 miles. The best tree specimens are found in Del Norte, Humboldt, and Mendocino Counties.

The Avenue of the Giants begins in Phillipsville, 250 miles north of San Francisco. From here, travelers can wind through 43,000 acres of Humboldt Redwoods State Park, or stop along the way to drive *through* a redwood at one of three commercially-run sites.

For tree watching at its best, visit the 106,000-acre Redwoods National Park between Crescent City and Eureka. A shuttle bus service departing from the information center in Orick takes visitors to Tall Trees Grove to see the world's tallest known tree, measured at 367.8 feet in 1968. The park includes more than 120 miles of trails through huge redwood groves. Hard-core tree lovers can travel north again to Del Norte Coast Redwoods and Jedediah Smith Redwoods State Parks near the Oregon border.

National Park Service GREAT BEACH

HIGHWAY ONE NORTH

No trip to California is complete without a visit to at least one portion of Highway One, the winding, spectacular, and in some places tortuous road that hugs most of the California coast from Oregon to Mexico.

Some of the most rugged and unspoiled coastline can be found north of the Golden Gate Bridge, starting with Great Beach at the Point Reyes National Seashore, just north of San Francisco (pg. 22). For 200 miles, the road twists and turns, traversing the high cliffs and sudden valleys.

Stop at Bodega Bay for a cup of clam chowder and see why Alfred Hitchcock chose this town to film *The Birds*. Gualala and Point Arena are also favorite getaway towns for San Franciscans. While swimming is ill-advised along much of the rocky coast, there are several state beaches as well as unmarked beaches along the way. A small parking lot jammed with cars is usually evidence of a trail leading to a secluded beach.

Travelers should not expect much in the way of amenities on this ride. But the sleepy coastal towns do offer cozy bed and breakfast inns and restaurants serving up crab, oysters, clams, and other delights of the sea. At Rockport, Highway One turns inland for more than 100 miles. But along a local road, visitors can explore the rugged "lost coast" from South Fork to Petrolia and Capetown.

National Park Service LASSEN PEAK

Stand Next To A Volcano At Lassen

Even though Lassen Peak is an active volcano, the last time it erupted was in 1917. In fact, it erupted 300 times between 1914 and 1917! Despite the volcano's recent dormancy, visitors to the park can still see boiling lakes, bubbling mud pots, hot springs, and cinder cones.

Located 50 miles east of Redding on Hwy. 44, Lassen Volcanic National Park is completely surrounded by the much larger Lassen National Forest, an area of unparalleled beauty and scores of mountain lakes.

Because of its volcanic activity, the area offers some interesting geologic curiosities. Subway Cave, for instance, is a 1/3-mile tube of hardened lava. Bring a flashlight and jacket for the self-guided tour. Spatter Cone Trail is a 1-1/2-mile self-guided walk through an eerie volcanic landscape. Hat Creek Rim is a 14-mile-long escarpment created when the earth ripped along a fault and was thrust up on one side.

Avid hikers, mountain bicyclists, and horseback riders should travel the Bizz Johnson Trail, a 26-mile saunter along an old railroad logging grade between Susanville and Westwood. The trail snakes through the rugged Susan River Canyon and surrounding mountains.

Trinity County Chamber of Commerce TRINITY ALPS

The Untamed Trinity Alps

Sprawling northern California is a massive, untouched expanse of mountains, lakes and rivers. It is largely uninhabited, making it a great place to explore the untamed outdoors. Redding, on I-5, three hours north of Sacramento, is the natural anchor to this wild area. From here travelers can easily access three nearby lakes created by the Central Valley Project. All three are perfect for sailing, canoeing, camping, and fishing.

Whiskey Lake, smallest of the three, is just west of Shasta, a town now preserved as a state historic park. Take a quick car ride to the town of Hayfork on Hwy. 3 for a look at the Natural Bridge, a 200-foot arch across a narrow canyon.

Shasta Lake, the largest man-made lake in the state, was created by the impressive Shasta Dam, with a spillway three times as high as Niagara Falls. Snow-capped Mt. Shasta looms behind the lake's 370 miles of shoreline. Several marinas rent boats for a day or week. Nearby Shasta Caverns are accessible by diesel-powered catamaran. The ferry service operates year round from its harbor, 20 minutes north of Redding on I-5.

Clair Eagle Lake, just north of Weaverville, is long, narrow and less popular but just as spectacular as its nearby cousins. For an awe-inspiring drive through the Salmon-Trinity Alps Wilderness to Arcata on the Pacific coast, take Hwy. 299 from Redding.

The Beauty of Lake Tahoe

Even though technically a portion of the lake lies in Nevada, Lake Tahoe is California's jewel. At 6,227 feet above sea level, it is cradled in the granite setting of the High Sierra, 98 miles northeast of Sacramento and 45 miles southwest of Reno.

Many travelers are amazed at the clarity of the deep, blue water. The lake's average depth is 989 feet--1645 feet being its deepest point--and the water is 99.7% pure. With a surface area of 193 square miles, the lake holds enough water to cover the entire state of California 14-1/2 inches deep. On the Nevada side are the casinos, and all around is boating, hiking, biking, scenery, and skiing in abundance.

A car tour around the lake makes a great day trip. From I-80, take Hwy. 89 south past Truckee, an Old West town once famous for its lawlessness and saloons. Stop at the Donner Memorial State Park, a monument to a party of pioneers caught in the cruel winter of 1846-47 and driven to insanity and cannibalism.

Continue south on 89 past a number of state parks, perfect for picnicking or camping. Vikingsholm is a 38-room granite castle on Emerald Bay, built in the style of a Norse fortress, and one of many mansions on the lake.

Emerald Bay is the visual highlight of tour. A short hike past Eagle Falls offers an unparalleled view of the lake. Fanette, its only island, is crowned with a stone tea house. Mansion enthusiasts should continue the short distancc to Tallac Historic Site Estates, to tour a number of prestigious mansions built in the late 19th century and later.

The swimming is great on Baldwin, Pope, and Regan Beaches on the south edge of the lake. A cruise into the town of South Lake Tahoe makes a nice stop for lunch or dinner. Those feeling lucky can drive a few more miles to Stateline in Nevada, where the serenity of the Lake is shattered by the glitter of casino lights.

Continuing north on Hwys. 50 and 28, the next stop is the Ponderosa Ranch. That's right, travelers can tour Ben Cartwright's ranch house just as it was in "Bonanza's" first episode in 1959. In summer the ranch hosts pony rides and a petting farm for kids, along with action-packed gunfights and hay wagon breakfasts.

Traveling north again, past Crystal Bay, and its north shore casinos, travelers re-enter California at Kings Beach. This is a center for sailing, water-skiing, rafting, and kayaking. A number of marinas rent boats or paddleboats, and offer lake tours for larger groups. One marina in Kings Beach even offers a kayak brunch.

Tahoe North Visitors & Convention Bureau LAKE TAHOE

There's also plenty to do for the culturally inclined. On the north and south shores of the lake are cultural festivals and daily special events, including rodeos, air shows, art shows, craft fairs, farmers markets, jazz concerts, and an annual Shakespeare Festival. In spring and fall, travelers can hike, bike, parasail, or ride horseback. Leaf peepers can get a great look at the fall colors from a hot-air balloon.

Squaw Valley, the famed ski resort, takes travelers on a 2,000-foot vertical ride aboard the Squaw Valley Cable Car to the new High Camp Bath and Tennis Club, elevation 8200 feet. Up top are ice skating, tennis, swimming, hiking, horseback and mountain bike riding, and--for the highly adventurous--bungee jumping.

A favorite ride for mountain bikers is the Flume Trail, which begins at Spooner Lake State Park, just northwest of Hwys. 50 and 28 in Nevada.

The north shore of Lake Tahoe boasts eight golf courses and the south shore five. There are plenty of public tennis courts, world-class restaurants, and shops in and out of the casinos.

With 212 ski lifts, an average annual snowfall of 500 inches, and mild daytime temperatures, skiing conditions around Lake Tahoe are near perfect. There's also plenty of snow for cross-country skiers and snowmobilers.

Grass Valley and Nevada County Chamber of Commerce PANNING FOR GOLD

THE MOTHER LODE

In the early days, gold could be found by turning over rocks in a riverbed and plucking out the nuggets. Modern travelers to the region's many streams and seven major rivers can still search for flakes of glitter. Gold Country is a 200-mile stretch of Sierra foothills, extending from Grass Valley and Nevada City in the north to Oakhurst and Raymond in the south. The entire route is traversed by Hwy. 49, appropriately called "The Gold Chain." Oakhurst, with its false front buildings, stone courthouses, and Gold Rush museums, is typical of the Old West towns along the highway.

Next travel north through Mariposa and Colterville. Well-preserved Jamestown is where such movies as *High Noon* and *Butch Cassidy and the Sundance Kid* were filmed. Railtown 1897 SHP, near the edge of town, contains the rolling stock of the Sierra Railroad. Columbia, two miles past Sonora off Hwy. 49, also has been restored as a state historic park, vintage 1860s.

Farther north is Angels Camp, the locale for Mark Twain's *Celebrated Jumping Frog of Calaveras County*. The towns of San Andreas, Jackson, Sutter Creek, and Diamond Springs offer more Gold Rush thrills. Historic Nevada City, developed as an inland retreat for wealthy families from San Francisco, offers horse-drawn carriage rides, an Art Deco courthouse, and several bed & breakfast inns. Grass Valley is home to Empire Mine SHP, site of the oldest, richest, hardrock gold mine in California. In operation from 1850 until 1956, an estimated 5.8 million oz. of gold were extracted from 367 miles of underground passages.

National Park Service YOSEMITE VALLEY

Experience Unique Yosemite

Teddy Roosevelt called it the most beautiful place on earth, and many of the 3,000,000 annual visitors to Yosemite agree. The park boasts 200 miles of primary roads and 750 miles of trails. Popular Yosemite Valley accounts for only 1% of the park's 1,170 square miles, but is home to many waterfalls and such legendary formations as Half Dome and El Capitan.

Other sites offer beauty all their own. Glacier Point, accessible from Hwy. 41, offers an overlook with a commanding view of Yosemite Valley. For sweeping views of the Sierra, take Tioga Pass Rd., a 39-mile drive that crosses Tuolumne (TWAL-o-me) Meadows, the largest sub-alpine meadow in the Sierra.

The Mariposa Grove of Giant Sequoias is located 36 miles south of Yosemite Valley via Hwy. 41. Activities include hiking and ranger-led walks. From here, travelers can walk to the Grizzly Giant which, at 2,700 years, is considered the oldest of all the sequoias.

Summer traffic is heavy at Yosemite, but the park provides complimentary shuttle bus service. Yosemite Valley offers more than 1,200 rooms, cabins, and tent cabins; reservations are a must. A wilderness permit is required for overnight stays in Yosemite's back country. In winter, Badger Pass Ski Area, the oldest in California, offers beginner and intermediate skiing, as well as 90 miles of cross-country trails.

National Park Service SEQUOIA PARK

The Big Trees

Sequoia National Park is one of the few places on earth where, in a span of 45 miles, travelers can ascend from 1,700 feet to 14,494 feet. Along with adjacent Kings Canyon National Park, Sequoia offers much of the beauty of Yosemite with a fraction of the crowds.

Accessible via Hwy. 180 from Fresno or Hwy. 198 from Visalia, the two parks range from the brushy foothills of the San Joaquin Valley to the barren peak of Mt. Whitney, highest point in the continental United States. The 46-mile General's Highway is the primary road that connects the two parks. More than 1,000 miles of trails cut through a magnificent display sequoia groves, granite mountains, and glacial lakes.

Sequoia, is home to 4 of the world's 5 largest sequoia trees, including one called General Sherman. At 102.6 feet girth and 274 feet in height, it is the largest known living tree on earth. The General Grant, in Kings Canyon National Park's Grant Grove, is a few feet thicker but not as tall.

The Congress Trail Loop, an easy 2-mile hike, winds past groups of Sequoias. At Tunnel Log, travelers can drive under a fallen giant. Crystal Cave shelters unusual geological formations, and breathtaking Moro Rock offers a 360 degree view of the Sierra and surrounding valleys.

Lake Oroville District SYCAMORE COVE

Boating On Lake Oroville

Just a few miles from the town of Paradise is Lake Oroville State Recreation Area, one of the premier boating lakes in the state. Man-made Lake Oroville is located on the Feather River, where California's central valley meets the Sierra foothills. The area is about an hour's drive from Sacramento on Hwy. 70, then east on Hwy. 162.

It is the lake's shape--a spidery mass of crooked forks--that makes it a mariner's delight. With 167 miles of shoreline, boaters can explore hidden coves and canyons while enjoying warm temperatures and the distant vistas of Plumas National Forest. Lime Saddle and Bidwell Canyon Marinas rent boats. In the spring, mariners can travel within a quarter mile of 640-foot Feather Falls.

The Feather River Fish Hatchery, located below the dam on Table Mountain Blvd., is open for tours. It's particularly delightful during autumn when the salmon and steelhead run. Special windows give visitors a unique view of fish leaping their way up the ladder to the hatchery. The lake is a mecca for anglers since it is stocked annually with trout, bass, catfish and salmon.

Hikers can enjoy the Feather Falls Hiking Trail, a moderate 3.5-mile walk to an observation platform overlooking Feather Falls. The Oroville Dam, 770 feet high and 3,000 feet thick at its base, is the highest earth-filled dam in the United States. An exhibit at the visitor center tells the story of the dam's construction.

Dave Henry, Sacramento CVB RIVERBOAT DELTA KING

SACRAMENTO: A CAPITAL TIME

Ninety minutes northeast of San Francisco, Sacramento is a river town built on the confluence of the American and Sacramento Rivers. Both provide hundreds of miles of waterways for fishing, swimming, and rafting in the lazy style of Huck Finn. Travelers can view several replica paddle-wheel river boats permanently docked in town, a testament to the days when Sacramento was a bustling supply center for Gold Rush prospectors. For a self-guided tour of Sacramento's earliest settlement, visit Sutter's Fort at 27th and L Sts.

The Sacramento Zoo houses more than 700 animals in open-air grottoes, islands, and other natural settings. It is located in William Land Park, which also includes a 6-acre playground, golf course, fairy-tale town, and picnic and sports facilities. Old Sacramento is a 28-acre national historic landmark with more than 100 restored and re-created buildings from the 19th century. Railroad buffs can visit the California State Railroad Museum, largest of its kind, at the corner of 2nd and I Sts. For old car fans, there's the Towe Ford Museum on Front St., home to the most complete collection of antique Fords in the world.

The Crocker Art Museum, oldest public art museum in the west, boasts a fine collection of European paintings. The Victorian Governor's Mansion, home to California's governors through Ronald Reagan, is now a museum of 19th century culture.

Demi DeSoto BLOSSOM TRAIL

Fresno County's Blossom Trail

California's grand central valley is to agriculture what Hollywood is to entertainment. For a fragrant tour of some of the finest fruit orchards in the region, drive the 67-mile Blossom Trail starting in Fresno.

With the snow-capped Sierra Nevada as a backdrop, travelers can catch the Blossom Trail on Hwy. 41 north to Ashlan Ave. in Fresno. Follow the pink and blue "Blossom Trail" signs around the full-circle tour.

While the drive is always scenic, it is especially beautiful in the spring, when the pink, red, and white blossoms of almond, apricot, plum, peach, nectarine, and apple trees appear. The first stop is Centerville, a once-prosperous community turned into a ghost town when residents denied the railroad passage in 1887. Traveling east on 180 offers a view of the tall mountains of Sequoia & Kings Canyon National Parks.

Turning south on Hwy. 63 and west on Manning, brings travelers to the town of Reedley. Take a few moments to visit the Mennonite Quilt Exhibit and gaze at the grandest mansions in Fresno County.

Continuing through some of Fresno County's 1.3 million agricultural acres, visitors may notice many of the tree trunks are painted white. This helps prevent scorching of trees by the hot sun. The full circle tour can be completed in two to six hours depending on stops.

San Francisco Convention & Visitors Bureau TEA GARDEN

Golden Gate Park

Once a wasteland of shifting sand dunes, Golden Gate Park is one of today's preeminent urban parks in the world. Stretching more than 30 city blocks, the park is home to museums, arboretums, gardens, and a number of hiking and biking trails.

The 1017-acre park is located between Baker St. on the east and the Pacific Ocean on the west. The big cultural attractions are the Asian Art Museum, the California Academy of Sciences, M.H. de Young Memorial Museum, the Japanese Tea Garden, and the Conservatory. Travelers can buy a single pass to the five sites, all within walking distance of each other.

There are at least two dozen recreational opportunities in the park, including a 9-hole golf course and 21 tennis courts. Boat and bicycle rentals are available at Stow Lake and there's also an exquisitely restored working carousel at Children's Playground. Riding lessons are offered at the Golden Gate Park Stables. Bike and roller skate rentals are available at a number of shops along Lincoln and Stanyan Sts.

The best way to see the park is on foot or bicycle. Start at the Music Concourse. Travel west through the many foot trails to Stow Lake and on to the Buffalo Paddock near 36th Ave. for a rare look at a bison herd.

Santa Cruz County Conference & Visitors Council BOARDWALK

SANTA CRUZ'S BOARDWALK

Before the likes of Disneyland and Universal Studios, there were good old-fashioned amusements parks like the one in Santa Cruz. California's only operating beach front amusement park, the Beach Boardwalk is a cornerstone of Santa Cruz history and culture.

The classic 1911 carousel and the Giant Dipper roller coaster are National Historic Landmarks. Other attractions include more than 25 rides, a vast old-time arcade, shops, and restaurants. The park is adjacent to the beach, so sunbathing is an additional option.

Santa Cruz, located at the northern tip of Monterey Bay, is hugged by redwood forested mountains. It's the epitome of the California beach community, with sun-drenched surfers and bikini-clad sun bathers. Another Santa Cruz must is a ride on The Roaring Camp and Big Trees Railroad. The historic narrow gauge train leaves the wharf regularly for the 2-hour journey through the magnificent San Lorenzo River Canyon.

For more Santa Cruz fun, try the Mystery Spot on North Branciforte Drive. Here, where the laws of gravity appear to be reversed, balls roll uphill and visitors find themselves leaning at precarious angles.

The Municipal Wharf on Beach St. is a hot spot for pier fishing. Enjoy a meal, then stroll along the pier and watch the sea lions, pelicans, and passing boats. Deep sea fishing trips, excursions, and bay cruises depart regularly from the Wharf.

National Park Service POINT REYES LIGHTHOUSE

Walk The Earthquake Trail

Travelers crossing into Point Reyes National Seashore, just 35 minutes north of San Francisco, are also crossing over the San Andreas Fault--from one major tectonic plate to another. San Francisco, along with the rest of the U.S., is on the North American plate. Point Reyes is on the very eastern edge of the Pacific plate. The slow movement of the two plates in opposite directions is the cause of much earthquake activity in the Bay Area.

Whether it's the result of geology or some other force, Point Reyes is a place of rare beauty and fragility. The Bear Valley Visitors Center, just off Highway One near Olema, was the epicenter of the great 1906 earthquake. This is a good spot to begin the tour. The Earthquake Trail is a .7-mile walk (also wheelchair accessible) along the San Andreas Fault. It's one of several self-guided tours that highlight everything from earthquake geology, to estuary life, to the migration patterns of the gray whales.

From Bear Valley, turn left on Limantour Rd., 8 miles to Limantour Beach, a good spot to wade, watch birds, beach comb, or picnic. The lighthouse at the very tip of Point Reyes offers a fantastic view of the Pacific. On a clear day, travelers can see the distant Farallon Islands. Inland Tomales Bay gives another view of ocean life. Marshall Beach, a short walk from the parking lot, is a great place for children to swim, since there are calmer waters on the bay side of the park.

San Francisco Convention & Visitors Bureau CABLE CARS

San Francisco Magic

Travelers with only one day to visit San Francisco should see the city via its famous 49-mile drive. This tour doesn't cover all of San Francisco, but it takes in the major scenic, historic, and cultural attractions as well as a taste of some of its cozy neighborhoods.

The planned route is well marked by blue and white sea gull signs. Begin any place along the drive; a good spot is the city's Civic Center at Van Ness and Hayes. The drive goes through Japantown, the posh shopping district of Union Square, colorful Chinatown, and chic Nob Hill. Stop on Telegraph Hill and take public transit to Coit Tower for one of the city's best views. Those who like gift shops and seals should stop either at Pier 39 or Fisherman's Wharf.

The 49-mile drive bypasses crooked Lombard Street, but a detour onto Russian Hill will rejoin the drive near Fort Mason where it runs along San Francisco's famed Marina district, hit hard in the 1989 earthquake.

Next, it's down to the beaches and the zoo, up through Golden Gate Park, and on to the top of Twin Peaks, one of the highest points in San Francisco. Continue to Mission Dolores for a taste of the city's Hispanic neighborhood. This drive, with stops, takes the entire day and shows the best San Francisco has to offer.

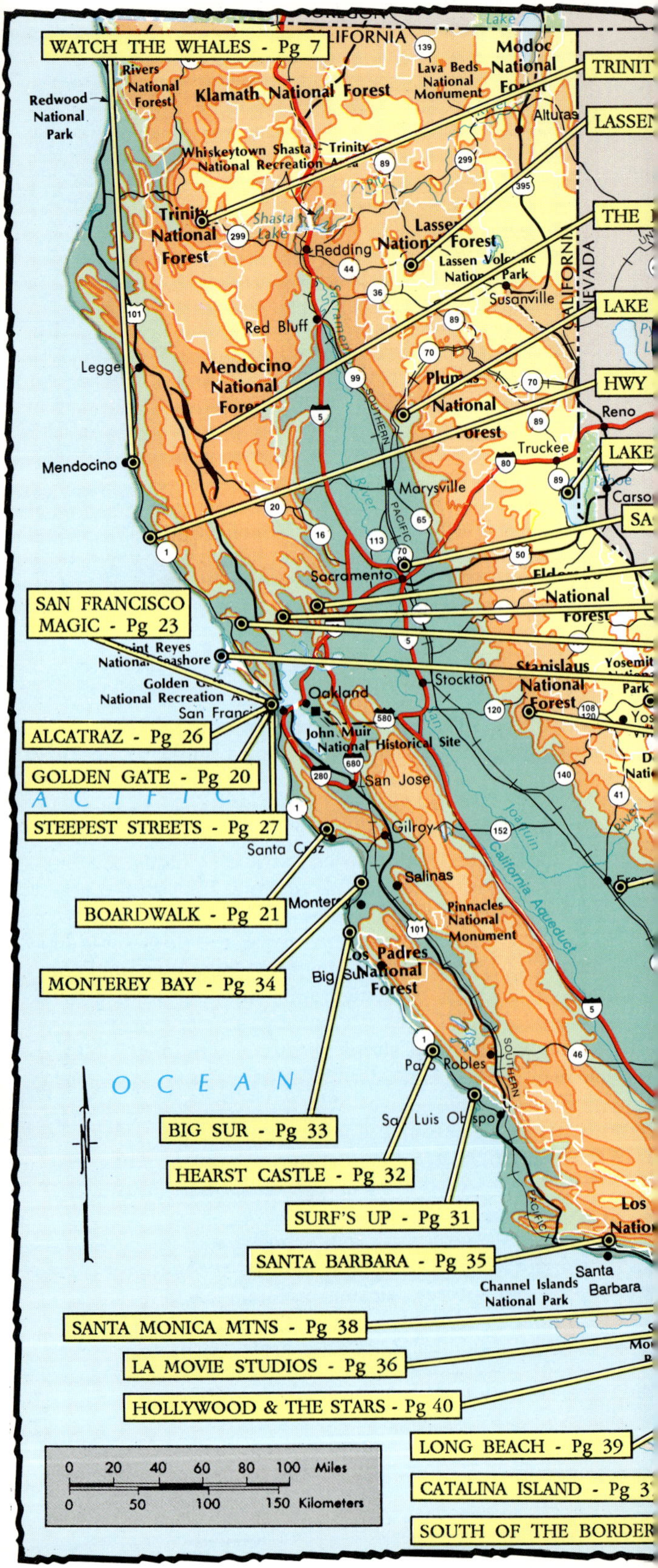

WATCH THE WHALES - Pg 7
SAN FRANCISCO MAGIC - Pg 23
ALCATRAZ - Pg 26
GOLDEN GATE - Pg 20
STEEPEST STREETS - Pg 27
BOARDWALK - Pg 21
MONTEREY BAY - Pg 34
BIG SUR - Pg 33
HEARST CASTLE - Pg 32
SURF'S UP - Pg 31
SANTA BARBARA - Pg 35
SANTA MONICA MTNS - Pg 38
LA MOVIE STUDIOS - Pg 36
HOLLYWOOD & THE STARS - Pg 40
LONG BEACH - Pg 39
SOUTH OF THE BORDER
CALIFORNIA
Redwood National Park
Klamath National Forest
Lava Beds National Monument
Modoc National Forest
Alturas
Whiskeytown Shasta - Trinity National Recreation Area
Trinity National Forest
Shasta Lake
Redding
Lassen National Forest
Lassen Volcanic National Park
Susanville
Red Bluff
Mendocino National Forest
Plumas National Forest
Mendocino
Reno
Truckee
Marysville
Sacramento
National Forest
Stockton
Oakland
John Muir National Historical Site
San Jose
Stanislaus National Forest
Gilroy
Santa Cruz
Salinas
Pinnacles National Monument
Los Padres National Forest
Big Sur
Paso Robles
California Aqueduct
O C E A N
Channel Islands National Park
Santa Barbara
0 20 40 60 80 100 Miles
0 50 100 150 Kilometers

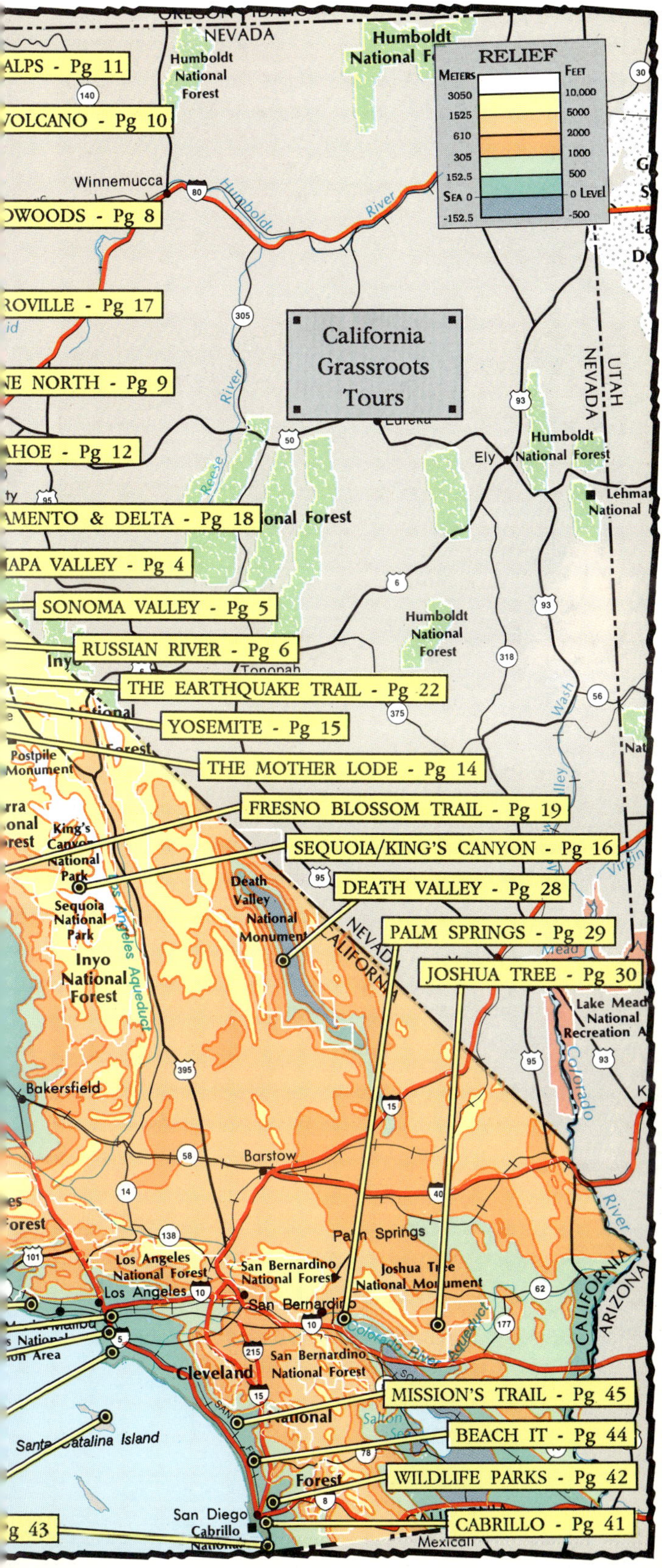
California
Grassroots
Tours
RELIEF
Meters
Feet
3050
10,000
1525
5000
610
2000
305
1000
152.5
500
Sea 0
0 Level
-152.5
-500
ALPS - Pg 11
VOLCANO - Pg 10
DWOODS - Pg 8
ROVILLE - Pg 17
NE NORTH - Pg 9
AHOE - Pg 12
AMENTO & DELTA - Pg 18
APA VALLEY - Pg 4
SONOMA VALLEY - Pg 5
RUSSIAN RIVER - Pg 6
THE EARTHQUAKE TRAIL - Pg 22
YOSEMITE - Pg 15
THE MOTHER LODE - Pg 14
FRESNO BLOSSOM TRAIL - Pg 19
SEQUOIA/KING'S CANYON - Pg 16
DEATH VALLEY - Pg 28
PALM SPRINGS - Pg 29
JOSHUA TREE - Pg 30
MISSION'S TRAIL - Pg 45
BEACH IT - Pg 44
WILDLIFE PARKS - Pg 42
CABRILLO - Pg 41
g 43
NEVADA
Humboldt National Forest
Winnemucca
Humboldt River
Reese River
Ely
UTAH
NEVADA
Lehman
Devils Postpile Monument
King's Canyon National Park
Sequoia National Park
Inyo National Forest
Los Angeles Aqueduct
Death Valley National Monument
NEVADA
CALIFORNIA
Lake Mead National Recreation Area
Colorado River
Bakersfield
Barstow
Palm Springs
Los Angeles National Forest
Los Angeles
San Bernardino National Forest
San Bernardino
Joshua Tree National Monument
Colorado River Aqueduct
Cleveland National Forest
Santa Catalina Island
San Diego
Cabrillo
Mexicali
CALIFORNIA
ARIZONA

California Office of Tourism ALCATRAZ

Lock Yourself In At Alcatraz

One of the highlights of a trip to San Francisco is the ferry ride to one of its most famous landmarks, Alcatraz. Once the prison home of such notorious criminals as Al Capone and The Bird Man of Alcatraz, the federal prison was officially closed in 1963.

Today Alcatraz is part of the Bay Area's 74,000-acre Golden Gate National Recreation Area. Access to the 12-acre island is free, but there is a ferry fee. The Red & White Fleet boats cast off at 30-to 45-minute intervals from Pier 41 at Fisherman's Wharf. Reservations are highly recommended.

On the island, travelers can take a tour of the main prison block with its steel bars, claustrophobic (9 x 5-foot) cells, mess hall, library, and "dark holes" where inmates were sent for solitary confinement. Tour guides will be happy to close one of the steel-plated doors behind any unruly visitor, to dramatize the sense of complete isolation.

The island offers great views of the Golden Gate Bridge, nearby Angel Island, and San Francisco, 1-1/4 miles away. Those who listen closely will hear, as the prisoners did more than 30 years ago, the laughter of the revelers on Fisherman's Wharf.

San Francisco Convention & Visitors Bureau A STEEP ONE

San Francisco's Steepest

When you're traveling the streets of San Francisco and encounter a traffic sign that reads "Hill," believe it. San Francisco has 42 hills and at least two are traversed by streets with a gradient greater than 30%. (In comparison, a steep mountain pass has a 7% grade). Ready for some adventure? Here are the steepest streets in San Francisco in descending order:

1. & 2. Filbert between Leavenworth and Hyde; 22nd St. between Church and Vicksburg, both 31.5%.

3. Jones between Union and Filbert, 29%.

4. Duboce between Buena Vista and Alpine, 27.9%

5. & 6. Jones between Green and Union; Webster between Vallejo and Broadway, both 26%.

7. & 8. Duboce between Divisadero and Alpine; Duboce between Castro and Divisadero, both 25%.

9. Jones between Pine and California, 24.8%.

10. Fillmore between Vallejo and Broadway, 24%.

Rules of the road: go slowly, pump your brakes, keep your eyes open.

Don't miss Lombard St., billed as the most crooked street in the world, with 9 hairpin turns in a single block. There's an old saying about the City by the Bay, "When you get tired of walking around San Francisco, you can always lean against it."

National Park Service DANTE'S VIEW

Death Valley Wildflowers

Think it gets hot in Death Valley? Look at some of its place names: Stovepipe Wells, Furnace Creek, Dante's View, Badwater Basin. Yet if the fall and winter rains are plentiful, a blanket of spring wildflowers will cover the huge desert park annually. There are more than 900 plant species here. February to June is the best time to catch the colorful show of Desert Bear Poppy, Cacti, Mariposa Lily, Lupine, Mojave Wildrose, Paintbrush, and Mojave Desert Rue, to name a few.

The monument hugs California's border with Nevada, approximately 150 miles northwest of Las Vegas and 300 miles northeast of Los Angeles. Precipitation is sparse, with an average annual rainfall of only 1.9 inches. Summertime temperatures can reach 120-125 degrees.

In addition to the flowers, travelers will find a magnificent array of other flora, fauna, wildlife, and geologic formations. Badwater on the valley floor, 282 feet below sea level, is the lowest spot in the Western Hemisphere, yet it is within 90 miles of Mount Whitney (14,495 feet), the highest point in the contiguous U.S.

Many features in the monument can be reached by car from the Furnace Creek Visitor Center. Here, travelers can choose a number of 1- to 4-hour drives to places like Natural Bridge, a relic of an ancient waterfall, or Artists Drive, a 9-mile route through the color-splashed Black Mountains, or the intriguing man-made Scotty's Castle off Hwy. 267.

Palm Springs Aerial Tramway THE TRAM

Take A Tram Above Palm Springs

Palm Springs, "America's Desert Playground," is known for its celebrity residents, superb golf courses, and sunny, hot weather. Located 107 miles east of Los Angeles, the city of Rolls Royces and swimming pools boasts 354 days of sunshine.

One of the best ways to see this desert oasis is from the Palm Springs Aerial Tramway. A dramatic ride on Swiss-style cable cars takes travelers from the desert floor to a mountain station 8,516 feet above sea level in Mt. San Jacinto State Park and Wilderness Area.

The tram, the world's largest single-span lift, departs at half hour intervals during daylight hours year-round. The ride covers 12,800 feet with a vertical ascent of 5,873 feet--more than a mile. The two 80-passenger enclosed cars travel on 11 cables weighing 330 tons.

Up top is a gift shop and observation area, as well as 54 miles of hiking trails, five campgrounds, and the Nordic Ski Center, open in winter. The highlights of the trip are views of Palm Springs and the desert that stretch for 75 miles. To reach the ride from Palm Springs take Hwy. 111 to Tramway Rd.

National Park Service JOSHUA TREE NAT. MON.

The Praying Arms Of The Joshua Tree

The poetically named Joshua Tree is actually a giant member of the agave family, attaining heights of 30 feet. It got its name, the story goes, due to its upstretched branches, which reminded Mormon pioneers of Joshua beckoning people to the promised land.

The Joshua Tree symbolizes the beauty and richness of the Mojave desert that stretches from Palmdale, just north and east of Los Angeles, into Nevada. Joshua Tree National Monument is approximately 50 miles northeast of Palm Springs. There are park entrances on Hwy. 62 and I-10.

The monument's altitude ranges from 1,000 to 6,000 feet, the mighty Joshua trees growing at higher elevations in the central and western parts of the park. Take a self-guided nature tour to a palm oasis from monument headquarters in Twentynine Palms, or a car trip to the large boulders of Hidden Valley, once said to have been a convenient hideaway for cattle rustlers and other rogues of the West.

For sweeping vistas of both mountains and deserts, visit Keys View, a side trip off the main park route south of Hidden Valley. Or drive along the 18-mile 4WD Geology Tour Road past the relics of mines and stands of barrel cactus.

Monterey Visitor & Convention Bureau — ALONG HIGHWAY ONE

Surf's Up On The South Central Coast

California's coast from San Simeon to Ventura, a 200-mile drive, includes some of the state's finest beaches and picturesque towns. At the northern edge of this region is Morro Rock near the town of Morro Bay. Now a nesting ground for peregrine falcons, the rock is massive and daunting, but it competes with a large power plant built unceremoniously nearby.

Traveling south, San Luis Obispo is 12 miles inland on Highway One, a good place to get the feel of a mission town. Travel nine miles south again for a dip in the redwood hot tubs of the Sycamore Mineral Springs Resort near Avila Beach.

At this point Highway One travels inland for a lengthy course through Lompoc. Jalama Rd., 5 miles south of Lompoc, offers a chance to get away from the crowds via a country ride through canyons and valleys to a beautiful beach park on the coast.

In Santa Barbara, 10 miles south near Carpinteria, is the next best thing to the North Pole. Santa Claus Lane is a block-long stretch of gift shops, all featuring Christmas themes. Finally it's on to Ventura to visit San Buenaventura Mission on East Main St. or stretch out on the coastal beaches where the water is decidedly warmer than in the north.

Hearst Monument/John Blades FROM THE AIR

Roam The Hearst Castle

There is nothing quite like the lavish, legendary estate of the late publishing magnate, William Randolph Hearst. Tucked in the Santa Lucia Mountains, overlooking the Pacific Ocean and Highway One, it is now accessible to the public as a State Historical Monument. It took craftsmen nearly 28 years to create the 165-room mansion and to cultivate the 127 acres of gardens, terraces, pools, and walkways.

La Casa Grande is the name given to the main house. It has 14 sitting rooms, a billiard room, theatre, library, a kitchen bigger than most homes, and a wine cellar with 3,000 bottles of rare European vintages and California wines. In addition to the main house, the estate includes indoor and outdoor pools, tennis courts, and three guest houses, the largest of which is 20 rooms on three levels.

The Castle is open every day except Thanksgiving, Christmas and New Year's. It takes *four* 1/2-mile tours to see the mansion and grounds completely. Each tour takes about 2 hours and covers one area of the estate. In addition to four day tours, evening tours are available in spring and fall. Reservations are recommended.

Monterey Visitor & Convention Bureau BIG SUR

THE REMARKABLE BIG SUR

For a 90-mile stretch between Carmel in the north and Sam Simeon in the south, Highway One roams through one of the most spectacular stretches of scenery in the world--Big Sur. Flanked by the Santa Lucia Mountains and the rocky Pacific coast, the Big Sur is not a destination tourist attraction. There are no large towns or villages, no golf courses or shopping malls, and only 1500 permanent residents. But there are plenty of high cliffs and grassy promontories dotted with wildflowers.

While amenities are few, there is an abundance of camping, hiking, fishing, and swimming. Garipata Beach is a local favorite for swimming, and campers flock to Julia Pfeiffer Burns, Pfeiffer Big Sur, and Andrew Molera State Parks.

With a good pair of binoculars, travelers can sight the California gray whales from late November to early February as they head south to their breeding grounds. The whales' return trip north runs from February through April, but the whales tend to travel farther out at sea on the northbound leg.

The offshore area has been declared a refuge for California sea otters, which live contentedly on the abundant kelp beds. Bird watchers should keep a lookout for the California brown pelican, the red-billed oystercatcher, golden eagles, owls, valley quail, and kingfishers.

Monterey Bay Aquarium THE AQUARIUM

TOUR MONTEREY BAY & 17 MILE DRIVE

The cypress-covered Monterey Peninsula is crowded with natural and cultural wonders from its southern edge in chic Carmel to the town of Monterey, site of the famous Monterey Bay Aquarium. Carmel, home of Clint Eastwood, is at the southern entrance of the popular 17-Mile Drive.

This toll route takes travelers past some of the world's most spectacular seascapes, 6 world-class golf courses including Pebble Beach, palatial estates, and the natural beauty of the Del Monte Forest. At the northern end of the drive is "Butterfly City, USA." Each autumn millions of orange and black monarch butterflies migrate here from faraway Alaska and Mexico.

Monterey is a bustling tourist port. Here are Fisherman's Wharf and the famous Cannery Row, immortalized by John Steinbeck when the region was the sardine capital of the world. At Cannery Row travelers can visit the spectacular 216,000-square-foot aquarium, offering a fascinating look at the undersea world of Monterey Bay, one of the richest marine environments in the world. The aquarium is home to more than 6,500 sea creatures including the popular sea otters. Among the other area attractions is the new Maritime Museum of Monterey. Located in Monterey's historic Custom House Plaza, the museum features priceless and unique artifacts and exhibits relating to the region's maritime history.

Santa Barbara Convention & Visitors Bureau THE COUNTY COURTHOUSE

TAKE THE SCENIC DRIVE AROUND SANTA BARBARA

There are two ways to tour this year-round resort town of soap opera fame. The Red Tile Walking Tour is a 12-block journey through the city's charming downtown. The 15-mile Scenic Drive (maps available in town) gives travelers a sweeping tour of greater Santa Barbara.

The Scenic Drive starts at the illustrious courthouse on Anacapa St. Climb the 85-foot clocktower for a panoramic view. Next is El Cuartel-El Presidio de Santa Barbara, the Historical Museum, and The El Paseo--an Old Spanish-style shopping arcade. At the nearby Santa Barbara Museum of Art, travelers can view of the works of O'Keefe, Hopper, Chagall, Pisarro and others. The Museum of Natural History houses the giant skeleton of a blue whale and exhibits on prehistoric Indian life.

Mission Santa Barbara with its twin bell towers is a Catholic parish church open to the public year round. Santa Barbara's Botanic Gardens are devoted entirely to the study of California's native flora. The city also has a superb zoo. Nearby Stearns Wharf is the oldest operating wharf on the west coast.

For the architecturally-minded, this tour includes two historic homes, the 14-room Victorian Fernald House and the Trussel-Winchester Adobe, built with adobe bricks, timber, and brass from a wrecked ship. The finale, at Yacht Harbor and the Hope Ranch Residential Area, shows travelers why Santa Barbara residents would never dream of leaving.

Universal Studios UNIVERSAL STUDIOS

Movie Making In L.A.

For an inside view of L.A.'s legendary entertainment industry in action, take a day-long excursion through the back lots and special effects stages of Universal Studios, Warner Bros. Studios, or Paramount Pictures.

Universal Studios, the world's largest television and motion picture facility, is located in Universal City, right off Hwy. 101. The box office is open daily. True to its name, at Universal you'll cruise the galaxy with the crew of the starship *Enterprise*. See what it's like to experience an 8.3-magnitude earthquake and a "Backdraft" fire. Then take a narrated train ride through 420-acres of famous sets.

Warner Bros. Studios on Hollywood Way in Burbank is less glitzy than Universal. Guides lead 10 to 12 persons through sound stages, a $20-million wardrobe inventory and back lots. The 2-hour tour leaves twice daily, six days a week.

Tours at Paramount Pictures on Melrose Ave. in Hollywood are on a first come basis. Arrive early at the visitor center on Gower Street for the 2-hour weekday tours. You may be able to squeeze Warner and Paramount tour into one tour, but leave an entire day to experience the extravaganza of Universal Studios.

Santa Catalina Island Company AVALON BAY

CRUISE TO CATALINA ISLAND

Few automobiles are allowed on beautiful Catalina Island, 26 miles across the sea from Long Beach and San Pedro harbors. But public transportation is available for a number of tours of island highlights. Travelers will find sandy beaches, clear blue waters, and hidden harbors reminiscent of the Mediterranean.

Five cruise companies provide frequent daily departures to the island from Long Beach, San Pedro, and Newport Beach, which take 1 to 2 hours, depending on the point of departure. San Diego and Oceanside take 3 to 4 hours.

Once in Avalon, the island's main port, travelers can stroll through the charming town or investigate water sports. Enthusiasts can jet ski, paddle board, kayak, parasail, scuba dive, snorkel, and (of course) swim. Glass bottom boat tours of a nearby cove, known as the "undersea garden," provide a magnificent display of marine plant life and colorful fish. A nature conservancy and the Wrigley Memorial and Botanical Garden are showplaces for native island plants.

The island's Art Deco casino, made famous during the 1930s and 1940s, once attracted the biggest names in Hollywood and the Big Bands of the era. The tour includes the Avalon theatre with its rare pipe organ, and the Casino ballroom, a 180-foot circular dance pavilion with no interior columns.

California Office of Tourism SANTA MONICA MOUNTAINS

Drive The Curves Of The Santa Monica Mountains

The beach town of Malibu is famous as a Hollywood hideaway and a mecca for tanned surfers. But it is also gateway to the Santa Monica mountains, a patchwork of state, federal, and private parks, reserves, and ranches that offers incomparable views of the ocean, mountain scenery, and some exhilarating driving experiences.

The Santa Monica Mountains are accessible from Hwy. 101, but the most scenic entry is from Highway One. Take Topanga Canyon Blvd. just east of Malibu. The road winds its way up the mountain with a series of narrow, hairpin turns. At the top is the famous Mulholland Hwy. Go left and follow this scenic corridor west along the spine of the mountains for some 50 miles.

The drive offers city panoramas of the San Fernando Valley and the Los Angeles Basin, as well as sweeping vistas of the ocean. There are plenty of places to stop, hike, and camp in the mountains. A number of north/south roads, such as Kanan Rd. and Malibu Canyon Rd., take travelers from Mulholland back to Malibu, with many good beach stops along the way.

Long Beach Area CVC SHORELINE VILLAGE

HISTORIC LONG BEACH

California's fifth largest city is a favorite embarkation point for boaters and fisherman. Land lovers can also view some spectacular architecture here. The Ocean Center Bldg. at 110 W. Ocean Blvd. is an example of Mediterranean Revival. A shield of sea shells highlighted by Neptune's face decorates the entrance. At 101 Pine Ave. is the First National Bank Bldg., built in 1906. Notice the building's Italianate pediments, terra cotta cornice, and famous clock tower.

For a taste of Art Deco, continue on Pine to the Bradley Bldg. with its brilliant terra cotta tile work. Across the street is the triple-gabled Pacific Coast Club, one of Long Beach's oldest. Cross 3rd St. to the Farmers and Merchants Bank, opened in 1922. The historic interior remains intact, complete with the original teller cages and hardware.

To see Spanish Revival, walk south from Long Beach Plaza to the elaborate ornamentation of the Breakers Hotel, 210 E. Ocean Blvd. Go east on Ocean Blvd. to the Villa Rivera, an international design winner when it opened in 1929. The 16-story building has an extended V-shape of reinforced concrete with more of its mass below the ground than above. Complete the tour by walking Shoreline Dr. to Shoreline Village for a look at a 1906 carousel, the only remnant of the once mighty Pike Amusement Park.

Los Angeles CVB — HOLLYWOOD

Explore Tinsel Town

There are just as many ways to see Tinsel Town as there are legends about it. From a comfortable seat in a Graveline Tours Cadillac hearse, travelers can see the spot where George "Superman" Reeves shot himself, where John Belushi overdosed on drugs and where other Hollywood legends came to their inglorious deaths.

The Capitol Records tower, at the famous corner of Hollywood and Vine, is designed to look like a stack of records topped with a stylus. The El Capitan Theatre, site of the world premiere of *Citizen Kane*, has been completely remodeled with an art deco interior. The revamping of the El Capitan is part of an upgrade for the newly named 8-block Cinema District.

Don't miss Mann's Chinese Theatre on Hollywood Blvd. for a look at the hand and foot prints of Hollywood's legends, as well as imprints of Betty Grable's leg, Jimmy Durante's nose and Donald Duck's webbed feet. The Walk of Fame extends more than 3 miles along Hollywood Blvd. from Gower St. to Sycamore Ave., the terrazzo commemorating nearly 2,500 film greats.

At the Hollywood Wax Museum on the Boulevard, travelers can see replicas of their favorite stars in wax. Those who pine for the days when films had no sound track can visit the Silent Movie Theater near the Fairfax District. Renovated in 1991, this is the only known silent movie house in the world, complete with a vintage organ.

National Park Service THE OLD LIGHTHOUSE

See The Tidepools At Cabrillo National Monument

Cabrillo National Monument, at the southern tip of Point Loma in San Diego, is one of the smallest national monuments in the country. But don't let its size fool you. The monument is home to a teeming city of tidepool life.

On the western side of the park, where the ocean meets the land, is a rocky environment of marine plants and animals that have adapted to harsh tidal conditions. Here are the flowery anemone, the scavenging shore crab, grazing limpets, spongy dead man's fingers, and hundreds more species that look strangely unfamiliar. The glassed-in observatory at the monument is a great place to view the Pacific gray whale migration in winter.

For a casual hike, try the Bayside Trail. Along it is a unique example of a coastal chaparral forest, as well as remnants of a coastal artillery system built to defend San Diego harbor during World Wars I and II. Another landmark is the old Point Loma lighthouse, the beacon that welcomed sailors to the pretty bay from 1855 to 1891.

To reach the monument take Rosecrans St. (SR 209) south. Turn right on Canon St., left onto Catalina Blvd., and then proceed through the Naval Ocean System Center gates to the end of the point.

Sea World of California SHARK TANK

KISS A WHALE IN SAN DIEGO

San Diego is home to three world-class wildlife parks, any of them a full-day trip. Sea World on Mission Bay is a wonderland of aquariums, exhibits, and shows. But the undisputed draw is the killer whale team of Shamu and Baby Shamu. The pair performs daily before delighted (and wet) crowds. Here, too, travelers can see the world's largest collection of live sharks, 350 penguins, and a walrus pool.

Sea World is but one attraction on the 4,600-acre Mission Bay, a multi-island playground of beaches, boat-launching ramps, picnic areas, campgrounds, playgrounds, and golf courses. The world-renowned San Diego Zoo is in Balboa Park, the heart of San Diego. It's home to more than 4,000 animals including Sumatran orangutans and Chinese leopards. The zoo was one of the first in the world to replace cages with natural habitats.

Thirty miles north of San Diego, in Escondido, is the San Diego Wild Animal Park. The 2,150-acre park houses hundreds of animals native to Africa and Asia, which thrive in the San Diego climate. Hop a monorail for a bird's-eye journey into the wild, or walk along Kilimanjaro Trail or Gorilla Grotto. To reach the Wild Animal Park, travel north on I-15 and exit on Via Rancho Pkwy.

Bob Yarbrough

TIJUANA MARKET

South Of The Border

A popular trip from San Diego is the short jaunt across the border into Mexico. Tijuana, the first stop, is Mexico's most-visited city. Attempts to clean up the city's tawdry image have been only partially successful, but there is an unmistakable energy in Tijuana.

Travelers can shop for inexpensive Mexican gifts and handiwork, visit the Agua Caliente Racetrack on evenings and weekends, or see a bull fight during the summer. There's no need to convert American currency; dollars are happily accepted, but travelers should bring small bills.

Rather than drive to Tijuana, take the San Diego Trolley from downtown to the border, or walk across the border and catch a cab to the downtown section. Travelers who do drive should pick up a short-term insurance policy at the border, since most American insurance policies are invalid in Mexico.

The city-weary traveler can avoid border towns altogether by driving 70 miles south on Highway One to Ensenada, a resort town and sport fishing center on Todos Santos Bay. This laid-back town, the port of call for several cruise ships, boasts fine restaurants and shops. Estero Beach south of town is a favorite among swimmers and surfers.

To the south is Baja, an 850-mile stretch of desert and mountains. The roads aren't always in good repair, but travelers are rewarded with fantastic beaches as well as lovely towns and vistas.

City of Oceanside

OCEANSIDE PIER

Beach It In La Jolla

Along Highway One from north of San Diego to Oceanside is a delightful string of sandy beaches, charming towns, and sweeping vistas, worthy of a camera and swim suits. Start in the fashionable enclave of La Jolla, 15 minutes north of San Diego. Prospect St. is the main street in town, with rows of art galleries, boutiques, restaurants, and small hotels.

Drive 10 minutes up North Torrey Pines Rd. to a wind-swept 1,750-acre preserve of gnarled torrey pine trees, one of only two places where these trees grow. Walk along the marked paths among the preserve's cliffs and canyons, then down to 6 miles of gorgeous beaches. Just up the highway is the town of Del Mar, a mecca for thoroughbred racing fans during the summer. Del Mar offers more boutiques and galleries. Ballooning is a favorite activity, and several companies offer hot air flights.

The two towns of Encinitas and Leucadia afford more picturesque southern California vistas. Flower lovers can visit the Quail Botanical Gardens, east of Encinitas Blvd. Carlsbad, 10 minutes north, is famous for its mineral waters. Though the spring is inactive, the town is dotted with small hotels and spa facilities. Oceanside, the last city before the Camp Pendleton Marine base, has a 1900-foot pier, a favorite among fisherman. The restaurant at the end of the pier is a good place to watch the many races and regattas that take place here.

City of Oceanside MISSION SAN LUIS REY

FOOTSTEPS OF THE PADRES

Three of the most magnificent missions in California are located near San Diego: San Diego de Alcala, San Luis Rey, and San Juan Capistrano. Missions were central to the Catholic church's attempt to convert native Americans and colonize California. Whether the attempt was successful is hotly debated. But the beautiful missions are reminders of California's colorful, turbulent, past.

San Diego de Alcala was the first mission dedicated in what is now California. Founded by Father Serra in 1769, the mission was moved to its present site in 1774. Because it was the first of the California missions, it has been designated a basilica.

Mission San Luis Rey de Francia is one of only four missions still owned by the Franciscans, the loyal order that spearheaded the mission crusade up the California coast. Dubbed "King of the Missions," San Luis Rey once included 6 acres of buildings and supported 3,000 native Americans. The town is 5 miles east of Oceanside off S.H. 76.

Visiting San Juan Capistrano on March 19 gives travelers an opportunity to witness the famous and inspiring return of the swallows from their southern winter feeding grounds. This "Jewel of the Missions" was destroyed in the earthquake of 1812. Travelers can visit the Serra chapel and view the elaborate masonry of the Great Stone Church, now in partial ruins. Take Ortega Hwy. exit west from I-5 in San Juan Capistrano.

Redwood National Park

Names & Numbers

BIG SUR C OF C
Box 87
Big Sur, CA 93920
(408) 667-2100

WARNER BROS. STUDIOS
(818)954-1744

CABRILLO NAT. MONUMENT
P.O. Box 6670
San Diego, CA 92166
(619) 557-5450

CATALINA ISLAND C OF C
PO Box 217
Avalon, CA 90704
(310) 510-1520

DEATH VALLEY C OF C
118 Hwy 127, Box 157
Shoshone, CA 92384
(619) 852-4524

DEATH VALLEY NAT. MON.
Death Valley, CA 92328
(619) 786-2331

EUREKA C OF C
2112 Broadway
Eureka, CA 95501
(707) 442-3738

FRESNO C OF C
P.O. Box 1469
2331 Fresno Street
Fresno, CA 93716
(209) 233-4651

FT. BRAGG-MENDOCINO C OF C
P.O. Box 1141
Fort Bragg, CA 95437
(707) 961-6300

GOLDEN GATE PARK
(415) 666-7200

GOLDEN GATE PARK STABLES
J.F.K. Drive @ 36th Ave.
(415) 668-7360

GRASS VALLEY C OF C
248 Mill Street
Grass Valley, CA 95945
(916) 273-4667

GRAVELINE TOURS
(213) 876-0920

HEALDSBURG C OF C
217 Healdsburg Avenue
Healdsburg, CA 95448
(707) 433-6935

Redwood National Park

NAMES & NUMBERS

HEARST CASTLE
State of California
750 Hearst Castle Road
San Simeon, CA 93452
(800) 444-7275

JOSHUA TREE NAT. MONUMENT
74485 National Monument Drive
Twentynine Palms, CA 92277
(619) 367-7511

LAKE OROVILLE STATE RECREATION AREA
400 Glen Drive
Oroville, CA 95966
(916) 538-2200

LAKE TAHOE VISIT. AUTHORITY
P.O. Box 16299
South Lake Tahoe, CA 95706
(800) AT TAHOE

LASSEN VOLCANIC NAT. PARK
PO Box 100
Mineral, CA 96063-0100
(916) 595-4444

LASSEN NAT. FOREST
55 S Sacramento
Susanville, CA 96130
(916) 257-2595

LONG BEACH AREA C&V COUNCIL
One World Trade Ctr.-#300
Long Beach, CA 90831
(800) 4LB-STAY

LOS ANGELES C&V BUREAU
633 W Fifth St. - Suite 6000
Los Angeles, CA 90071
(213) 624-7300

MALIBU C OF C
23805 Stuart Ranch Rd.-#100
Malibu, CA 90265
(310) 456-9025

MONTEREY PENINSULA C OF C & V&C BUREAU
P.O. Box 1770
380 Alvarado Street
Monterey, CA 93942
(408) 649-1770

Tahoe North VCB LAKE TAHOE SKIERS

Names & Numbers

NAPA VALLEY CVB
1310 Napa Town Ctr.
Napa, CA 94559
(707) 226-7459

PALM SPRINGS TOURISM DIVISION
401 S. Pavilion Way
Palm Springs, CA 92262
(619) 778-8418; (800) 34-SPRINGS

PARAMOUNT PICTURES
(213) 468-5575

PT. REYES NAT. SEASHORE
Point Reyes, CA 94956
(415) 663-1092

REDDING C OF C
747 Auditorium
Redding, CA 96001
(916) 225-4433

RED & WHITE FLEET BOATS
Fisherman's Wharf
(415) 546-2628

SACRAMENTO CVB
1421 "K" Street
Sacramento, CA 95814
(916) 264-7777

SAN DIEGO CVB
1200 Third Avenue, Suite 824
San Diego, CA 92101-4190
(619) 232-3101

SAN FRANCISCO CVB
PO Box 429097
San Francisco, CA 94142-9097
(415) 391-2000

SAN LUIS OBISPO C OF C
1039 Chorro Street
San Luis Obispo, CA 93401
(805) 781-2777

SANTA BARBARA CVB
510-A State Street
Santa Barbara, CA 93101
(805) 966-9222

SANTA CRUZ COUNTY CVC
701 Front Street
Santa Cruz, CA 95060
(408) 425-1234

SEQUOIA NAT. PARK
(209) 565-3134

SONOMA VALLEY VB
453 First Street East
Sonoma, CA 95476
(707) 996-1090

SYCAMORE MINERAL SPRINGS RESORT
(805) 595-7302

TAHOE NORTH VCB
P.O. Box 5578
Tahoe City, CA 96145
(800) 824-6348

UNIVERSAL STUDIOS
(818) 508-9600

YOSEMITE NATIONAL PARK
P.O. Box 577
Yosemite, CA 95389
(209) 372-0265